Fun Facts

ABOUT THE

American Adventure

compiled by
Bruce and Becky Durost Fish

A Barbour Book

Fun Facts

ABOUT THE

American Adventure

© MCMXCVII by Barbour & Company, Inc.,

ISBN 1-57748-058-9

Published by Barbour & Company, Inc.
P.O. Box 719
Uhrichsville, Ohio 44683
http://www.barbourbooks.com

Member of the
Evangelical Christian
Publishers Association

Printed in the United States of America.

Did You Know...

While
Christopher
Columbus is
famous for his
1492 voyage, North
and South America are named for another explorer:
Amerigo Vespucci. He took two journeys to what is now
South America. After his second voyage in 1501-1502,
Amerigo was convinced he had discovered a New World.
In 1507, geographer Martin Waldseem proposed that this
New World be called America.

Chairman of the Board

Families during the early colonial period ate from a long board resting on trestles close to the fireplace. Rather than calling this a dining table, people called it the board table. If the family had a cloth to cover the table it was called a board cloth.

To sit at the board was to eat, and a hired hand expected both "room and board" as part of his pay. In the beginning, when smooth boards were hard to come by, the top of a packing case might be used. The family sat on benches, stools, or chests pushed up to the board. Many people didn't own chairs. If the family had one, it was reserved for the head of the house.

This is where we got the word chairman and the expression "chairman of the board."

Who Am I?

Match these names with the description
of what they discovered.

1. Vasco de Balboa   2. Ferdinand Magellan
3. John Cabot   4. Samuel de Champlain
5. Meriwether Lewis

A. Working with my partner, I discovered a
cross-continental route to the Pacific Ocean.

B. I explored the St. Lawrence River and founded the
settlement of Quebec. A large lake is named after me.

C. I crossed the Isthmus of Panama and discovered
the Pacific Ocean.

D. I explored what is now
Newfoundland, Nova Scotia, and
the New England coast.

E. I rounded the tip of South
America through
the strait now named for me.

5-A. Meriwether Lewis discovered the cross-continental route.
4-B. Samuel de Champlain explored the St. Lawrence River.
3-D. John Cabot explored Newfoundland.
2-E. Ferdinand Magellan rounded the tip of South America.
1-C. Vasco de Balboa discovered the Pacific Ocean.

I am....

Facts About Slavery

The first black slaves landed at Jamestown, Virginia, in 1619.

The first formal protest against slavery was made by Pennsylvania Quakers in 1688.

Slaves revolted in New York in 1712. Twenty-one were executed. Six committed suicide.

The First Fugitive Slave Act, which made it a crime to harbor an escaped slave or to interfere with a slave's arrest, was passed in 1793.

★★★

Importing slaves from other countries was outlawed in 1808, but about 250,000 slaves were imported illegally between 1808 and 1860, just before the Civil War broke out.

The Civil War broke out in 1861.

Nat Turner led a slave rebellion in Virginia in 1831.

Sojourner Truth, a former slave, began a speaking tour against slavery in 1843.

Frederick Douglas, a former/freed? slave, founded the North Star in 1847. This newspaper opposed slavery. The Dred Scot decision by the U.S. Supreme Court, which declared slavery to be legal, was made in 1857.

Slavery was abolished in Washington, D.C., in 1862.

Harriet Tubman freed 750 slaves in a raid in 1863.

Black prisoners of war were massacred by Confederate soldiers at Fort Pillow, Tennessee, in 1864.

The Civil War ended in 1865. That same year, the Thirteenth Amendment abolished slavery.

Flagging It

The flag of the United States was officially born in 1777 when the first Continental Congress "Resolved, that the Flag of the United States be thirteen stripes alternate red and white, that the Union be thirteen stars white on a blue field, representing a constellation."

As states were added, both stars and stripes were added to the flag until April 4, 1818 when Congress voted to keep the number of stripes at 13 and to add a star to the field for every new state. New stars are added on the July 4th after each state's admission to the Union. Stars have been added to the flag 26 times, the last time on July 4, 1960 when the star for the 50th state, Hawaii, was added.

The White House flag is flown from sunrise to sunset, but only when the President is in residence. The flag at the Capitol building is flown all night long, lit by lights from the Capitol dome. The flag should be saluted when it passes in a parade or review, is being raised or lowered, or is present at the playing of the national anthem or when the Pledge of Allegiance is said. Salute by standing at attention and placing your right hand over your heart. Men and boys should remove their hats and hold them over their left shoulders with their right hand. Many people recommend that women and girls do the same if they are wearing baseball caps or some other informal hat.

I Pledge Allegiance

The original Pledge of
Allegiance was written
in 1892 by Francis Bellamy.
It didn't contain the words
"under God" for another
sixty-two years. In 1954, an Act of Congress
added the phrase, and the Pledge has remained
the same ever since:

I pledge allegiance to the flag
of the United States of America,
and to the Republic
for which it stands,
one nation
under God,
indivisible,
with liberty
and justice
for all.

Period News

President Harry S Truman
didn't put a period after
his middle initial.

Do you know why?

✸✸✸

Answer:
The S in President Truman's name isn't an initial.
His middle name is simply the letter S.

The Top Ten

The Bill of Rights was adopted in 1791 and includes the first ten amendments to the U.S. Constitution. How many of the rights that are protected by this important document can you list?

1. _____

2. _____

3. _____

4. _____

5. _____

6. _____

7. _____

8. _____

9. _____

10. _____

ANSWERS

And the Answer Is...

Here are the rights
we are guaranteed by the ten
Amendments included in the
Bill of Rights.

1. Freedom of religion, speech, and the press, as well as the right to gather in groups and to ask the government to right wrongs.

2. The right to keep and bear arms.

3. A household cannot be forced to provide shelter for a soldier during peace time, and can only be made to do so during war in a way which follows the law. For decades, colonists had been upset by having to host British troops in their homes.

4. The right to be protected against unreasonable searches and seizures of our persons, houses, papers, and effects.

5. The right to a jury trial; the right not to be tried again for a crime which a person has already been found not guilty of; the right to not testify against ourselves in a criminal case; the right to have fair compensation for the value of any private property that is taken for public use.

6. The right to a speedy and public trial by an impartial jury; the right to face the witnesses against us; to be able to require people to testify for us; and to have a lawyer assisting in our defense.

7. The right to a trial by jury.

8. The right to protection from excessive bail, excessive fines, and cruel and unusual punishment.

9. Rules of construction of the Constitution.

10. Power not given to the federal government is granted to the individual states or to the people as long as the federal government has not prohibited such action.

First
Chimney
Sweeps

In Colonial America,
brooms were used to clean short chimneys,
but they didn't work well for tall chimneys.
To solve that problem,
many people would drop a chicken or two
down the chimney.
The birds' frantic wing beating
cleaned the chimney quickly.

Thirteen Originals

Can you list the thirteen original colonies?
They became the first states in the United States and
are remembered on our flag by the thirteen stripes.

1. _____

2. _____

3. _____

4. _____

5. _____

6. _____

7. _____

8. _____

9. _____

10. _____

11. _____

12. _____

13. _____

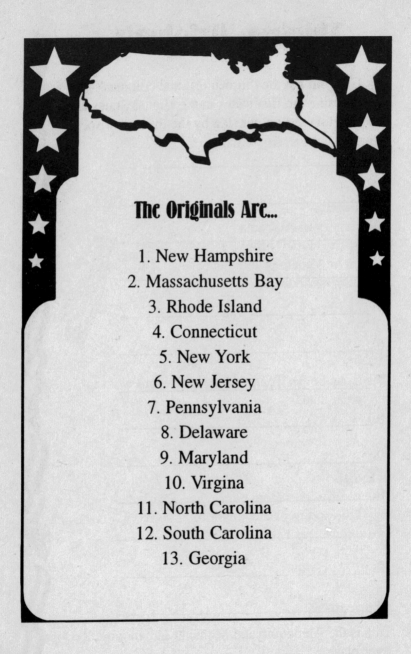

The Originals Are...

1. New Hampshire
2. Massachusetts Bay
3. Rhode Island
4. Connecticut
5. New York
6. New Jersey
7. Pennsylvania
8. Delaware
9. Maryland
10. Virgina
11. North Carolina
12. South Carolina
13. Georgia

What's in a Name?

Half of the names
of our states come from
Native American words:

Alabama
The territory of Alabama
became the home of the
Alabam or Alibamon Indians of
the Creek confederacy.

Alaska
This name comes from the Aleutian word alakshak, meaning "great land."

Arizona
This name comes from either the Pima Indian word meaning "little spring place" or from the Aztec word arizuma
meaning "silver-bearing."

Connecticut
This is the Algonquin and Mohican Indian word for "long
river place."

Hawaii

Many believe this is an English adaptation of the native word hawaiki or owhyhee, meaning "homeland."

Idaho

Many believe this name comes from the Kiowa Apache word for the Comanche.

Illinois

From the Algonquin word, illini, meaning "men" or "soldiers."

Iowa

From the Sioux word, ouaouia, meaning "one who puts to sleep."

Kansas

From the Sioux word, kansa or kaw, meaning "people of the south wind."

20

Kentucky

From the Indian word meaning "dark and bloody ground," "meadow land," or "land of tomorrow."

Massachusetts

A word meaning "large hill place," Massachusetts is the name of the tribe of Indians who lived near Milton.

Michigan

Probably from the Chippewa word micigama, meaning "great water," after Lake Michigan.

Minnesota

From the Sioux description of the Minnesota River, "sky-tinted water" or "muddy water."

Mississippi

Probably from the Chippewa words mici (great) and zibi (river).

21

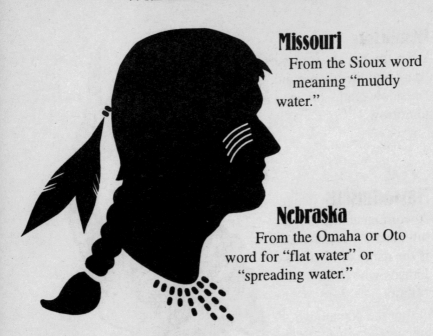

Missouri
From the Sioux word meaning "muddy water."

Nebraska
From the Omaha or Oto word for "flat water" or "spreading water."

North and South Dakota
From the Sioux word meaning "friend" or "ally."

Ohio
From an Iroquois word meaning "great," "fine," or "good river."

Oklahoma
The Choctaw Indian word meaning "red man."

Oregon
Some believe this name comes from the Algonquin wauregan, meaning "beautiful water."

Tennessee

Named after the tanasi Cherokee villages on the Little Tennessee River.

Texas

From the Caddo Indian word for "friend" or "ally."

Utah

From the Navajo word utes, meaning "upper" or "higher" and used for a Shoshone tribe.

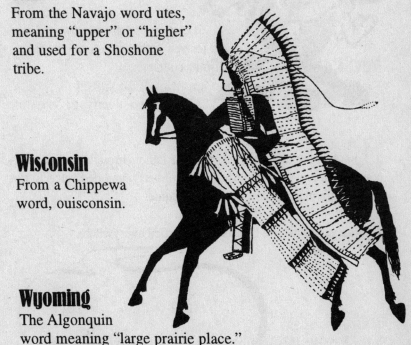

Wisconsin

From a Chippewa word, ouisconsin.

Wyoming

The Algonquin word meaning "large prairie place."

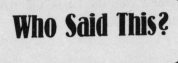

Who Said This?

Can you match the quote with the person who first said it?

A. Patrick Henry
B. John F. Kennedy
C. Martin Luther King Jr.
D. Abraham Lincoln

1. Ask not what your country can do for you but what you can do for your country.

2. Give me liberty or give me death.

3. Four score and seven years ago our fathers brought forth on this continent a new nation, conceived in liberty, and dedicated to the proposition that all men are created equal.

4. Injustice anywhere is a threat to justice everywhere.

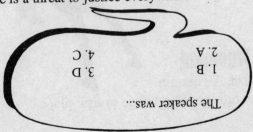

The speaker was...

1. B
2. A
3. D
4. C

24

Presidential Firsts

Our country has had 41 different men serve as president. Most of the presidents had different first names, but five first names show up more than once. One name was shared by five different presidents. Can you match the first names with the number of presidents who had them? Extra credit if you can name the presidents!

Andrew	5
George	4
James	4
John	2
William	2

Presidential Firsts Answered

Two presidents are named Andrew: Andrew Jackson, the seventh president, and Andrew Johnson, the seventeenth.

Two presidents are named George: George Washington, the first president, and George Bush, the forty-first.

Five presidents share the name James: James Madison, the fourth president; James Monroe, the fifth; James Buchanan, the fifteenth; James Garfield, the twentieth; and James (Jimmy) Carter, the thirty-ninth.

Four presidents are named John: John Adams, the second president; John Quincy Adams, the sixth; John Tyler, the tenth; and John F. Kennedy, the thirty-fifth.

Four presidents are named William: William Henry Harrison, the ninth president; William McKinley, the twenty-fifth; William H. Taft, the twenty-seventh; and William (Bill) Clinton, the forty-second.

Who's in Charge?

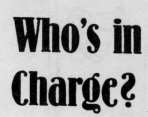

If the president of the United States died in office or was unable to do the job for some other reason (serious illness, surgery), we all know the vice-president would take office. But what if the vice-president was unable to do the job? Who would take office then? Listed below are the five positions that are used next to fill the office. Can you guess in what order those positions would be used?

_____ President Pro Tempore of the Senate

_____ Secretary of Defense

_____ Secretary of State

_____ Secretary of the Treasury

_____ Speaker of the House

The Answer Is...

Never in U.S. history has someone other than the vice president had to fill the office of the president. But if that situation arose, the office would be filled by these people in this order:

1. Speaker of the House

2. President Pro Tempore of the Senate

3. Secretary of State

4. Secretary of the Treasury

5. Secretary of Defense

We all know about the thirteen original colonies, but do you know which states were the last thirteen to be admitted to the Union?

1. _____

2. _____

3. _____

4. _____

5. _____

6. _____

7. _____

8. _____

9. _____

10. _____

11. _____

12. _____

13. _____

The Answer Is...

1. Hawaii—1959
2. Alaska—1959
3. New Mexico—1912
4. Arizona—1912
5. Oklahoma—1907
6. Utah—1896
7. Wyoming—1890
8. Idaho—1890
9. North Dakota—1889
10. South Dakota—1889
11. Montana—1889
12. Washington—1889
13. Colorado—1876

Who Made the Confederacy?

Eleven states left the Union during the Civil War. Here are their names, along with the date they left the Union.

1. South Carolina — December 20, 1860
2. Mississippi — January 9, 1861
3. Florida — January 10, 1861
4. Alabama — January 11, 1861
5. Georgia — January 19, 1861
6. Louisiana — January 26, 1861
7. Texas — February 1, 1861
8. Virginia — April 17, 1861
9. Arkansas — May 6, 1861
10. North Carolina — May 20, 1861
11. Tennessee — June 8, 1861

When Did They Come Back?

The Southern states were not automatically readmitted to the Union at the end of the Civil War. In some cases, it took several years. Here's the order in which the Southern states returned, along with the dates when they officially became part of the Union again.

1.	Tennessee	July 24, 1866
2.	Arkansas	June 22, 1868
3.	Alabama	June 25, 1868
4.	Florida	June 25, 1868
5.	Georgia	June 25, 1868 (also July 15, 1870)
6.	Louisiana	June 25, 1868
7.	North Carolina	June 25, 1868
8.	South Carolina	June 25, 1868
9.	Virginia	January 26, 1870
10.	Mississippi	February 23, 1870
11.	Texas	March 30, 1870

Keeping Count

*According to
the U.S. Census Bureau,
more than 266 million people
live in the United States,
and that population is growing.
After accounting for births, deaths,
people moving into the country,
and people leaving the country,
the Census Bureau reports
that the U.S. population
is growing by one person
every eighteen seconds.*

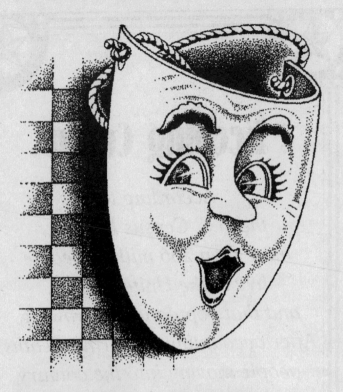

Who Am I?

Can you match the following
women's names with
what they did?

1. Clara Barton

2. Evangeline Cory Booth

3. Rosa Parks

4. Molly Pitcher

5. Sojourner Truth

6. Frances Willard

A. I was president of the Woman's Christian Temperance Union from 1879-1898 and fought for alcohol education, home protection, and voting rights for women.

B. I was arrested for refusing to give up my bus seat to a white person. This started the Montgomery, Alabama, bus boycott, one of the major events in the Civil Rights Movement.

C. I was the third of my parents' children to be placed in command of the Salvation Army in the United States.

D. I was born a slave. After I was freed, I gave speeches about the evils of slavery.

E. I was awarded a field commission by General Washington after I took charge of an artillery piece in a Revolutionary War battle when my husband was injured and couldn't continue fighting.

F. Because I gave medical help to injured soldiers during the Battle of Bull Run in the Civil War, I became known as the "Angel of the Battlefield." I founded the American Red Cross.

The Answer Is. . .

1-F: Clara Barton founded the American Red Cross.

2-C: Evangeline Cory Booth was placed in command of the Salvation Army in the United States.

3-B: Rosa Parks refused to give up her seat on the bus.

4-E: Molly Pitcher was awarded a field commission for taking charge of an artillery piece in a Revolutionary War battle.

5-D: Sojourner Truth gave speeches about the evils of slavery.

6-A: Francis Willard was president of the Woman's Christian Temperance Union.

For the Birds

Every state and
the District of Columbia
have a state bird.
Can you match these states
with their state birds?

Indiana	A. Willow goldfinch
Louisiana	B. Western meadowlark
Maine	C. Ruffed grouse
Montana	D. Roadrunner
New Mexico	E. Eastern brown pelican
Pennsylvania	F. Chickadee
Washington	G. Cardinal

Answers for the Birds

Indiana—Cardinal (G)

Louisiana—Eastern brown pelican (E)

Maine—Chickadee (F)

Montana—Western meadowlark (B)

New Mexico—Roadrunner (D)

Pennsylvania—Ruffed grouse (C)

Washington—Willow goldfinch (A)

A Royal State

Some of our states were named after
kings and queens of England and France. Can you guess
which states were named for the following people?

King George II of England

King Louis XIV of France

Queen Henrietta Maria
(wife of Charles I of England)

King Charles I of England
(there are two states named for him)

Queen Elizabeth I of England

The Answers Please...

Georgia...
is named for
King George II

Louisiana...
is named for
King Louis XIV

Maryland...
is named for Queen Henrietta Maria

North and South Carolina...
are named for King Charles I
(the Latin word Carolus means Charles)

Virginia...
is named for Queen Elizabeth I
(people in her day called her
the Virgin Queen because
she never married)

?

Fill in the Blanks

Can you add the missing consonants to these words so that they will spell the names of states?
(For example, __ __ O __ E I __ __ A __ __ would be RHODE ISLAND.)

A __ A __ A __ A

__ E __ __ __ Y __ __ A __ I A

__ I __ __ O __ __ I __

__ I __ __ I __ __ I __ __ I

__ E __   __ E __ I __ O

__ E __ __ O __ __

Time for a Promotion

Forty-five men have served as vice-president of the United States. Of those, only fourteen have eventually become president.

1. John Adams was vice-president under George Washington. He became our second president.

2. Thomas Jefferson was vice-president under John Adams. He became our third president.

3. Martin Van Buren was vice-president under Andrew Jackson. He became our eighth president.

4. John Tyler was vice-president under William Henry Harrison. He became our tenth president.

5. Millard Fillmore was vice-president under Zachary Taylor. He became our thirteenth president.

6. Andrew Johnson was vice-president under Abraham Lincoln. He became our seventeenth president.

7. Chester A. Arthur was vice-president under James Garfield. He became our twenty-first president.

8. Theodore Roosevelt was vice-president under William McKinley. He became our twenty-sixth president.

9. Calvin Coolidge was vice-president under Warren G. Harding. He became our thirtieth president.

10. Harry S Truman was vice-president under Franklin D. Roosevelt. He became our thirty-third president.

11. Richard M. Nixon was vice-president under Dwight D. Eisenhower. He became our thirty-seventh president.

12. Lyndon B. Johnson was vice-president under John F. Kennedy. He become our thirty-sixth president.

13. Gerald R. Ford was vice-president under Richard M. Nixon. He became our thirty-eighth president.

14. George Bush was vice-president under Ronald Reagan. He became our forty-first president.

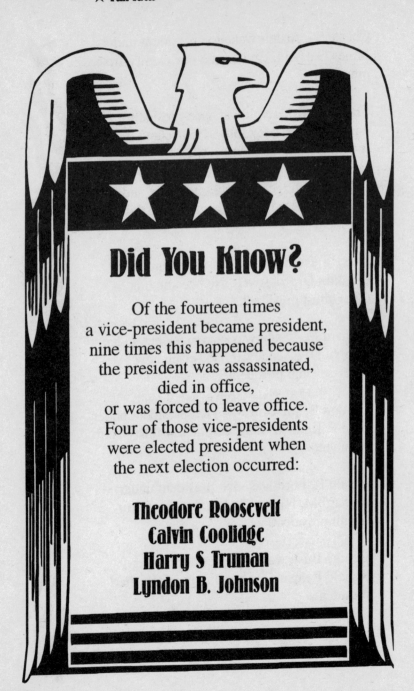

Did You Know?

Of the fourteen times
a vice-president became president,
nine times this happened because
the president was assassinated,
died in office,
or was forced to leave office.
Four of those vice-presidents
were elected president when
the next election occurred:

**Theodore Roosevelt
Calvin Coolidge
Harry S Truman
Lyndon B. Johnson**

On a Musical Note

"Hail to the Chief"
is the name of
the song played
when the president
of the United States
makes an appearance.

When the vice-president appears,
"Hail Columbia"
is played.

America's First Composer

The first important composer in America was William Billings, who lived from 1746-1800. He lived in Boston and tanned hides. As he got more business teaching singing and training choirs, Billings was able to give up his tanning business. Under William Billings, New England choirs began using pitch pipes. He also introduced the idea of having a cello accompany the singers. Before then, choirs had sung without accompaniment.

Two hundred years later choirs still sing songs by William Billings.

Famous Fires

Late one night,
when we were all in bed,
Mrs. O'Leary lit a lantern
in the shed.
Her cow kicked it over,
then winked her eye and said,
"There'll be a hot time
in the old town tonight."

While no one knows the true cause of the Chicago fire of October 8, 1871, the song about Catherine O'Leary and her cow lives on. The fire destroyed 1,750 buildings and burned four square miles of Chicago. Theories of what started the fire include a falling meteor, boys who were smoking, a neighbor of the O'Learys, and a drunken party-goer. The site on De Koven Street where the fire started is now occupied by a training facility for the Chicago Fire Department.

Other Famous Fires in American History Include:

August 24, 1814
White House and Other Government Buildings

British troops overran Washington, D.C., during the War of 1812 and deliberately set fire to the White House and other government buildings. With the help of Charles Carroll, First Lady Dolley Madison managed to escape the White House, carrying the silver, the red velvet curtains, and a portrait of George Washington. Legend has it that she was only a carriage-length ahead of the incoming British. The United States later won the war and peace was declared through the Treaty of Ghent.

★★★

April 18-21, 1906
The Great San Francisco Earthquake

The Great San Francisco Earthquake overturned stoves, crossed electrical wires, and broke containers of gas, causing four days of fire. Because the earthquake broke and twisted water pipes, most fire hydrants were dry. The fire department set off dynamite, pumped sewer water, and tried igniting black powder to stop the fires. Eventually, the fires burned 4.7 square miles of the city and caused about 275 million dollars worth of damage. Because the fires burned so hot, many bodies were never recovered, but the death toll was estimated to be between one thousand and fifteen hundred people.

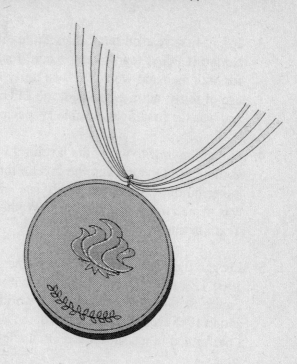

Try to identify the following American women sports stars:

1. In 1957 I became the first African-American woman to win the All-England women's singles championship at Wimbledon. I won two other major titles that year and was named Woman Athlete of the Year by the Associated Press.

2. I overcame polio as a child and was unable to walk properly until I was eleven years old. But in the 1960 Olympics in Rome, I won three gold medals in track: the 100 and 200 meter sprints and as anchor of the 4 x 100 meter relay team.

49

3. In my first year on the Ladies Professional Golf Association (LPGA) tour, I set a record for rookie earnings for both men and women. I won thirty-five titles by the age of thirty, am a member of the LPGA Hall of Fame, and was the first highly visible Hispanic woman athlete.

4. I taught myself to throw the javelin. I won gold medals at the 1932 Olympics in the javelin throw and the 80-meter hurdles, became a highly successful golfer, and was named the Associated Press Woman Athlete of the Year six times.

5. I began figure skating when I was nine years old, and in 1964 I won my first of five consecutive United States Figure Skating titles. I won three world championships and in 1968 won the gold medal at the Winter Olympics. I performed in ice shows and am a television commentator.

The answers are...

1. Althea Gibson
2. Wilma Rudolph
3. Nancy Lopez
4. Babe Didrikson
5. Peggy Fleming

Women Undercover

During the Revolutionary and Civil Wars, many women contributed by running farms and businesses, nursing, and working for aid organizations. But some women actually fought in the front lines.

Deborah Sampson

Deborah Sampson disguised herself as Robert Shurtleiff during the Revolutionary War. She enlisted in the Continental Army and fought in major battles. When she was injured, she treated her wounds herself to avoid detection. Although she was eventually discovered, she petitioned to keep her rank. After the war, she was given a soldier's pension and land.

Sarah Edmonds

During the Civil War, Sarah Edmonds disguised herself as a man and enlisted in the Union Army under the name Franklin Thompson. She fought at the Battle of Bull Run and became a spy "disguised" as a woman. She, too, was granted a pension after the war.

First States

Do you know which states fit these descriptions?

1. I take up the greatest amount of land.

_____

2. I have the biggest population.

_____

3. I make the most cheese.

_____

4. I produce the most apples.

_____

5. I am the only state that is an island.

_____

Answers:
1. Alaska
2. California
3. Wisconsin
4. Washington
5. Hawaii

Find the Capitals

Can you find the eighteen state capitals listed below? They may run forward, backward, up, down, or diagonally. Extra credit if you can identify the states these cities belong to.

```
I  N  D  I  A  N  A  P  O  L  I  S
N  A  O  J  U  N  E  A  U  N  N  E
D  S  V  W  G  E  E  B  I  R  I  N
I  H  E  A  U  I  O  L  E  D  T  I
A  V  R  A  S  S  A  I  E  H  S  O
I  I  A  U  T  S  L  A  T  H  U  M
P  L  M  O  A  E  P  M  E  L  A  S
M  L  N  I  P  I  E  R  R  E  O  E
Y  E  E  T  R  I  C  H  M  O  N  D
L  Y  N  A  B  L  A  E  S  I  O  B
O  O  T  N  E  M  A  R  C  A  S  M
M  B  A  T  O  N  R  O  U  G  E  B
```

Albany	Des Moines	Nashville
Augusta	Dover	Olympia
Austin	Helena	Pierre
Baton Rouge	Indianapolis	Richmond
Boise	Juneau	Sacramento
Boston	Montpelier	Salem

The State Capitals

Are...

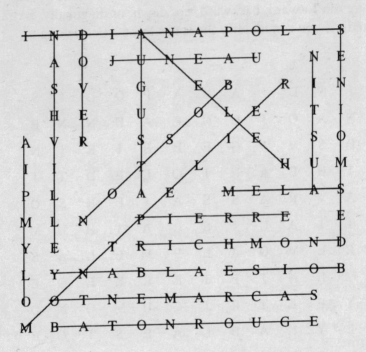

Albany, New York
Nashville, Tennessee
Dover, Delaware
Austin, Texas
Pierre, South Dakota
Indianapolis, Indiana
Boise, Idaho
Sacramento, California
Montpelier, Vermont

Des Moines, Iowa
Augusta, Maine
Olympia, Washington
Helena, Montana
Baton Rouge, Louisianna
Richmond, Virginia
Juneau, Alaska
Boston, Massachusetts
Salem, Oregon

see you at the polls

Who Can Vote?

When the United States was first founded, most voting laws required voters to be twenty-one years old or older, white males, and property owners. The changes in those laws that led to our current system took almost two hundred years. Do you know what changes were brought about by the following Amendments to the Constitution and Acts? Extra credit if you can correctly identify the decade in which the law took effect.

1. The 15th Amendment to the Constitution

2. The 19th Amendment to the Constitution

3. The Civil Rights Act

4. The Voting Rights Act

5. The 26th Amendment to the Constitution

Answers

The 15th Amendment

Prohibited citizens from being denied the right to vote because of race, color, or previously being a slave. (This took effect in 1870. Virginia, Texas, Mississippi, and Georgia were forced to ratify this amendment before they would be readmitted to the union.

The 19th Amendment

Gave all women the right to vote. (This took effect in 1920. Some people wanted it to give only white women the right to vote, but others fought for the inclusion of all women.)

The Civil Rights Act

Prohibited any attempts to prevent anyone from voting. (It took effect in 1957. Some states and communities had passed laws that made it almost impossible for African-Americans and other minorities to vote.)

The Voting Rights Act

Eliminated literacy and other voter tests. (It was passed in 1965. The next year, the percentage of eligible African-Americans who voted in the South increased from 28.6 percent to 47.5 percent.)

The 26th Amendment

Lowered the minimum voting age from twenty-one to eighteen. (Passed in 1971, this Amendment was a response to claims that if eighteen-year-old men could be drafted to fight in the Vietnam War, they should also be able to vote.)

Who Settled New England?

Many people think of the Pilgrims and those who settled the Massachusetts Bay Colony as farmers. While they had to farm once they arrived in the New World, most of them were anything but farmers when they lived in England and Holland.

Records show the occupation of 300 of those early settlers, and only 75 of them were farmers. The other 225 were weavers, tailors, coopers, shoemakers, and the like. Can you match these people with their profession?

John Alden	Professional soldier
William Brewster	Cooper (barrel maker)
John Carver	Village postmaster
Myles Standish	Printer

Answers:
John Alden was a cooper.
William Brewster (leader of the Pilgrims) was a village postmaster.
John Carver (first governor of Plymouth Plantation) was a printer.
Myles Standish was a professional soldier.

Quick Quiz

The Pilgrims noticed three big differences
between the land in Holland and
that in the New World.
Can you name them?

1. _____

2. _____

3. _____

The Pilgrims and other European settlers were struck by the abundance
of wood, the countless fast-running streams, and the seemingly limit-
less quantity of vacant land in the New World.

Answer:

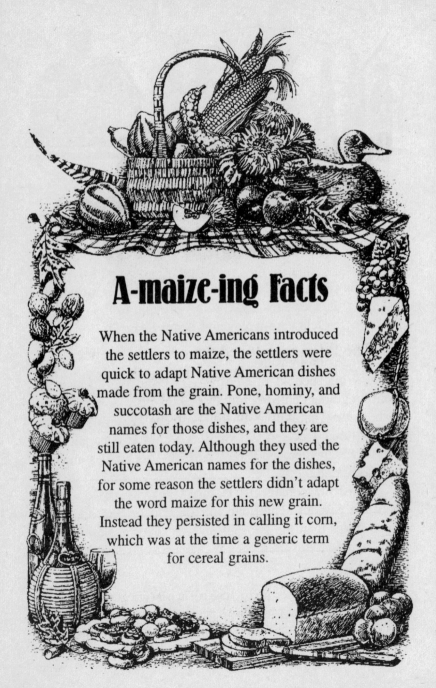

A-maize-ing Facts

When the Native Americans introduced the settlers to maize, the settlers were quick to adapt Native American dishes made from the grain. Pone, hominy, and succotash are the Native American names for those dishes, and they are still eaten today. Although they used the Native American names for the dishes, for some reason the settlers didn't adapt the word maize for this new grain. Instead they persisted in calling it corn, which was at the time a generic term for cereal grains.

How Swedes and Germans Helped English Settlers

Can you fill in the blanks with the three important things
the Germans and Swedes brought to the
Delaware valley and Pennsylvania?

The Swedes brought the _____ from
home. While people in New England and the Chesapeake
spent long hours constructing clapboard-sided houses similar
to those they had known in England, the English settlers in
Pennsylvania accepted the Swedish homes at once and lived
snugly within them until they had time to build something
more substantial.

English newcomers also learned how to use the _____
from the Swedes. This tool cut down trees and split them
much faster than the two-person saw that the English were
familiar with. But until they met the Swedish settlers, most
English hadn't seen this tool.

Germans and Swedes introduced the idea of a _____
_____. Jobs such as building homes, clearing
fields, and butchering livestock became day-long neighbor-
hood gatherings. Before, such jobs had taken days and weeks
and had been done by individual families.

61

Answers

The Swedes introduced the English to *log cabins* and *the axe*. The Germans and Swedes also showed the English how to have *work parties*.

Living High on the Hog

Hogs were an economical animal for early settlers to raise because they didn't have to give them special food. The hogs would go out into the woods and root around for food. Early settlers used every part of the hog—except its squeal! Because there were no freezers or refrigerators, the meat would be salted down to keep it from spoiling and then be stored in barrels. Meat from four good-sized hogs could carry a family through the winter. If for some reason the family saw the bottom of the pork barrel before spring arrived, they knew food would be scarce in the weeks ahead. This is the origin of the phrase "eating from the bottom of the barrel."

Corn

The Miracle Plant

To early English settlers, corn was a miracle plant. It made nourishing food for both people and animals. It was immune to most diseases that can destroy crops, and it was easy to raise. Corn took less than fifty days a year of a farmer's time and was easy to harvest. The yield per acre was about seven times that of wheat or barley.

No part of the corn plant went unused: the stalks provided winter feed for cattle; the husks were used to stuff mattresses; the cobs worked as tool handles and made good stoppers for jugs. Poultry thrived on corn kernels.

Taxing Matters

Sixteenth Amendment

There was no federal income tax
until after passage of the
Sixteenth Amendment
to the U.S. Constitution,
which took effect
February 25, 1913.

Great American Writers

Nine U.S. citizens have been awarded the Nobel Prize in Literature. Can you name any of them?

1. _____

2. _____

3. _____

4. _____

5. _____

6. _____

7. _____

8. _____

9. _____

Answers

1. Sinclair Lewis, 1930
2. Eugene O'Neill, 1936
3. Pearl S. Buck, 1938
4. William Faulkner, 1949
5. Ernest Hemingway, 1954
6. John Steinbeck, 1962
7. Saul Bellow, 1976
8. Isaac Bashevis Singer, 1978
9. Joseph Brodsky, 1987

Nailing It

Before the nineteenth century, when nails began to be made by machine, nails were expensive. Rather than use nails, builders would use wooden pegs to hold a house together. The pegs were carved from hardwood and then dried for a long time to prevent shrinking. Dried pegs were pounded into beams, and the ends were left sticking out. At the first sign of a wobbling rafter, the homeowner would pound the pegs in farther.

Go Fly a Kite

Everyone remembers the story of Benjamin Franklin using a kite in 1752 to show the electrical nature of lightning. But did you know that kites were used as early as 2500 B.C. in China?

Kites have been used for a number of purposes. A German book from the 1300s has an illustration of soldiers using a kite to drop a bomb on an enemy castle. Kites became popular as toys for children in the 1600s. And kites have been used to save lives. During the 1800s, shipwrecked boats used kites to carry lines to potential rescuers on shore.

The First Submarine

The first workable submarine was built during the Revolutionary War by David Bushnell. Built in Saybrook, Connecticut, the ship was about seven feet long and was called the Turtle because it looked like one. It was made from wood and powered by two propellers. After positioning the Turtle under an enemy ship, the pilot would spear the hull of the enemy ship with a screw that had a large time bomb attached to it.

The Turtle had three missions. In early September 1776, it was placed under British Admiral Richard Howe's flagship, but the bomb could not be deployed because the screw hit an iron bracket rather than the hull. During its second mission, the Turtle dove too deep and currents swept it away from its target. A third attack was prevented when the British guards challenged the pilot. The following morning, the Turtle's mother ship was sunk by the British, taking the Turtle with her.

Submarines in the Civil War

The Confederate Navy used an underwater boat they called a submarine. Men turned a hand crank to keep the propellors turning, and an air hose ran to the surface of the water so the crew could breathe.

Century of Invention

Can you match these inventions with their American inventors? They were all created between 1780 and 1880.

Articulating telephone	Alexander Graham Bell
Bifocal lenses	George Eastman
Cotton gin	Thomas Alva Edison
Incandescent light bulb	Benjamin Franklin
Long-distance steamboat	Robert Fulton
Reaping machine	Charles Goodyear
Roll film	Cyrus McCormick
Underwater telegraph cable	Samuel F. B. Morse
Vulcanization of rubber	Eli Whitney

And the Inventor Is...

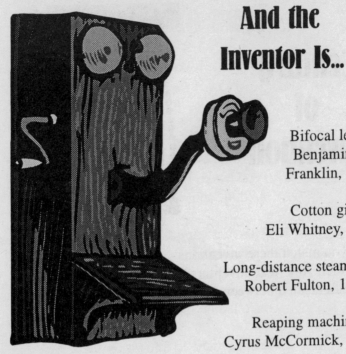

Bifocal lenses
Benjamin
Franklin, 1784

Cotton gin
Eli Whitney, 1793

Long-distance steamboat
Robert Fulton, 1807

Reaping machine
Cyrus McCormick, 1831

Vulcanization of rubber
Charles Goodyear, 1839

Underwater telegraph cable
Samuel F. B. Morse, 1842

Articulating telephone
Alexander Graham Bell, 1876

Incandescent light bulb
Thomas Alva Edison, 1879

Roll film
George Eastman, 1880

True or False

Do you know which of the following statements are true and which are false?

_____ 1. No two presidents have ever been related to each other.

_____ 2. Presidential inaugurations have always been held in January.

_____ 3. The first capital of the United States was Philadelphia.

_____ 4. The first white settlers to come to Oregon traveled on the Oregon Trail.

_____ 5. Connecticut is known as the Constitution State.

_____ 6. Maine was once part of Massachusetts.

_____ 7. Rhode Island was settled by people who wanted religious freedom.

_____ 8. Georgia was once a place where criminals were sent for punishment.

_____ 9. Martha Washington spent a winter in Valley Forge with Colonial troops during the American Revolution.

_____ 10. Alaska was once owned by Russia.

The Truth Is...

1. False   John Adams and John Quincy Adams were related, as were Theodore Roosevelt and Franklin Delano Roosevelt.

2. False   Inaugurations were originally held in March, which was also when the House of Representatives and the Senate began their sessions.

3. False   The first capital was New York City.

4. False   The first white settlers in Oregon were fur traders, followed by the military, and then a group of missionaries who settled Salem.

5. True   Connecticut is also known as the Nutmeg State.

6. True   Maine did not become a state until 1820.

7. True   Roger Williams and his followers left the Massachusetts Bay Colony so they could worship God the way they wanted to.

8. True   Georgia was originally a colony for prisoners.

9. True   Martha Washington helped care for the troops in Valley Forge.

10. True   Alaska was purchased from Russia in what was called at the time Seward's Folly because people thought Mr. Seward was crazy for wanting to buy the land.

Ordered States

Can you identify in what order the
thirteen original colonies became states?

Connecticut

Delaware

Georgia

Maryland

Massachusetts

New Hampshire

New Jersey

New York

North Carolina

Pennsylvania

Rhode Island

South Carolina

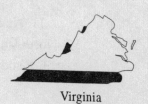

Virginia

73

In Correct Order

The original colonies were admitted as states in this order:

1. Delaware: December 7, 1787
2. Pennsylvania: December 12, 1787
3. New Jersey: December 18, 1787
4. Georgia: January 2, 1788
5. Connecticut: January 9, 1788
6. Massachusetts: February 7, 1788
7. Maryland: April 28, 1788
8. South Carolina: May 23, 1788
9. New Hampshire: June 21, 1788
10. Virginia: June 25, 1788
11. New York: July 26, 1788
12. North Carolina: November 21, 1789
13. Rhode Island: May 29, 1790

What's That Mean?

The years before the Civil War
are often called the
Antebellum Period.

The word *antebellum* comes
from two Latin words:
ante
which means before or in front of,
and
bellum
which means war.

So antebellum means
"before war."

What Did Slaves Do?

Most of us connect slavery with
working on cotton plantations,
but slaves did much more than work the land.
Can you think of some other jobs
that may have been given to slaves?

Answers:

Slaves in the South did a number of jobs. On plantations, they worked as butlers, maids, cooks, washerwomen, seamstresses, gardeners, coachmen, wagon drivers, stablehands, cowmen, pigmen, carpenters, masons, millers, smiths, shoemakers, spinners, and weavers. Off the plantation they worked in iron foundries and machine shops, were assistants to mechanics, carpenters, bakers and shop owners, cut wood for steamboats, and produced shingles, barrel staves, pickets, posts, and turpentine. They also were miners, mining gold in North Carolina, iron in Kentucky and Tennessee, and coal and salt in Virginia. They built roads and bridges and nearly all the railroad beds in the South.

Black Soldiers in the Civil War

Many white people thought black soldiers would not be able to fight well, and those black men who fought in the Civil War were paid only ten dollars a month, much less than white soldiers. But in spite of these prejudices, 178,975 blacks in 166 regiments fought in the Civil War. Stereotypes about black soldiers were addressed in an article in the March 28, 1863 New York Tribune:

> *Facts are beginning to dispel prejudices. Enemies of the Negro race, who have persistently denied the capacity and doubted the courage of the Blacks, are unanswerably confuted by the good conduct and gallant deeds of the men whom they persecute and slander. From many quarters comes evidence of the swiftly approaching success which is to crown what is still by some persons deemed to be the experiment of arming whom the Proclamation of Freedom liberates.*

The military didn't begin to be integrated until World War II. Even then, there were black-only units such as the Tuskegee Airmen, and often black soldiers were not given military honors that white soldiers received for similar acts of bravery.

Today, many people believe the military is one of the most integrated parts of American society. One of the most distinguished people to serve as chairman of the Joint Chiefs of Staff was General Colin Powell, an African-American who began his career in the army as part of the Reserve Officers Training Program.

Civil War Slang...

Some of the most
widely used expressions
by Civil War soldiers
included:

"let her rip,"

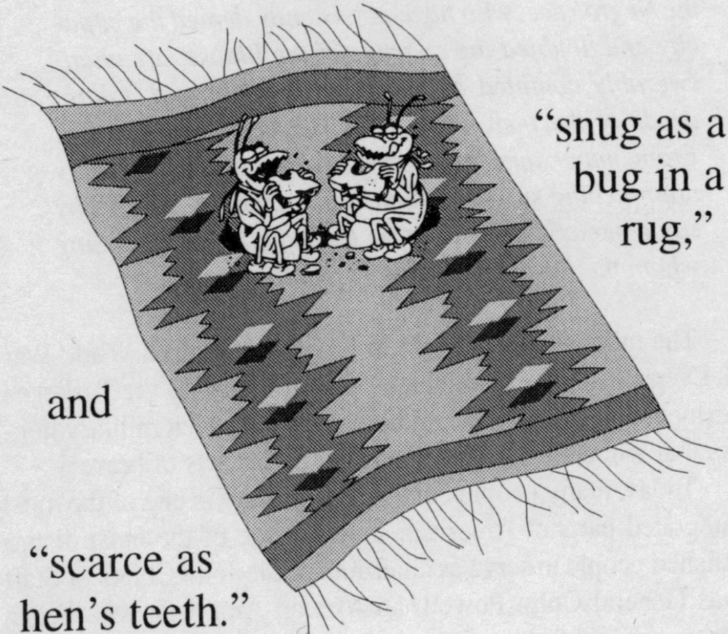

"snug as a
bug in a
rug,"

and

"scarce as
hen's teeth."

Civil War Nicknames

Can you guess the meaning of these nicknames that soldiers used during the Civil War?

1. Avalanche   _____

2. Doughboy   _____

3. Embalmed beef   _____

4. Johnny or Johnny Reb   _____

5. Lampposts   _____

6. Quaker guns   _____

7. Sawbones   _____

8. Torpedoes   _____

9. Virginia quickstep   _____

Nicknames Defined

1. Avalanche—A two-wheeled, springless ambulance cart that often made soldiers' injuries worse because of the rough ride it gave them.

2. Doughboy—A foot soldier. This name comes from the shape of the buttons on his uniform.

3. Embalmed beef—Tinned beef sold to the Union Army by Chicago meat packers.

4. Johnny or Johnny Reb—A Confederate soldier. After the war, Union soldiers were referred to as Billy Yank.

5. Lampposts—Artillery shells in flight. Soldiers called them lampposts because they looked like elongated blurs.

6. Quaker guns—Phony cannons built of logs that were painted black. These were used by the Confederate soldiers to fool the Union forces.

7. Sawbones—An army surgeon.

8. Torpedoes—Confederate Navy mines made of barrels, beer kegs, or old boilers that were filled with powder and suspended just under the water. Union soldiers once discovered a trainload of torpedoes and thought it was barrels of pork, so they rolled the barrels out of the train. The explosion could be heard for twenty miles.

9. Virginia quickstep—Union nickname for diarrhea, which was an all-too-common ailment during the war.

A Musical War

During the Civil War, both Confederate and Union camps were filled with music provided by bands and individual soldiers playing instruments such as harmonicas, fiddles, and banjoes. Both sides liked the songs *Home, Sweet Home* and *When This Cruel War is Over.*

Union Favorites

Yankee Doodle Dandy
Tramp, Tramp, Tramp
The Star Spangled Banner
John Brown's Body
revised to become
The Battle Hymn of the Republic

Confederate Favorites

Dixie
When Johnny Comes Marching Home Again
The Bonnie Blue Flag
The Yellow Rose of Texas

Famous Duels

Fighting with pistols at a pre-arranged time and place was a popular way to resolve "gentlemen's" disagreements in the 1800s. A sixteen-page pamphlet entitled "Code of Honor" was published by Governor John Lyde Wilson of South Carolina from 1838 to 1858. It presented the rules of dueling. Only about one in seven duels resulted in death or serious injury. Public outrage at the practice eventually led to its end. Here are some of the more famous duels:

Philip Hamilton
vs.
George Eacker
(1801)

The son of Alexander Hamilton, Philip was killed at the age of 19 in a duel between himself and George Eacker, a lawyer. They had argued over Hamilton's description of a speech made by Eacker.

Aaron Burr
vs.
Alexander Hamilton
(1804)

Three years after the death of his son in a duel, Alexander Hamilton was shot and killed by longtime political enemy Aaron Burr in a duel over Hamilton's criticisms of Burr's behavior.

Henry Clay
vs.
John Randolph
(1826)

Henry Clay was Secretary of State when he dueled with Senator John Randolph. The first shots missed their marks, and in the second round, Randolph's coat was struck by a bullet. "You owe me a coat, Mr. Clay," Randolph said. At that point, Clay and Randolph shook hands and stopped the duel. Both were unharmed.

Say. . ."I Do"

From the early days of Colonial America, American weddings have been quite varied. In those days:

Quakers...
held weddings in their meetinghouses and couples would marry themselves, often using their own vows.

The Dutch and Pennsylvania Germans...
were married in their native languages.

In the South...
weddings were usually held at home and were followed by card playing, dancing, and an elegant meal.

Congregationalists in New England...
didn't see marriage as a religious service because pagans also got married. So they made weddings a civil ceremony over-

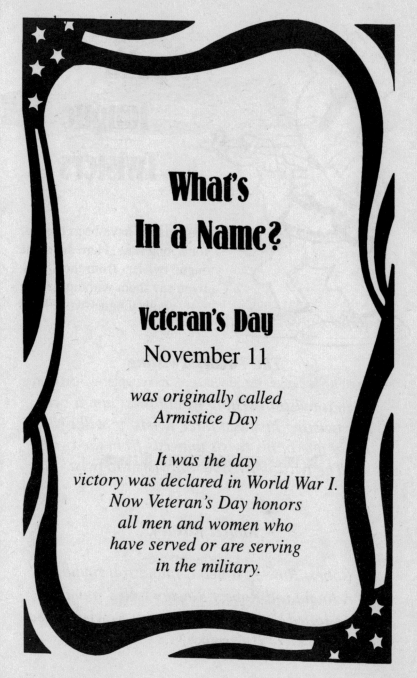

What's In a Name?

Veteran's Day
November 11

*was originally called
Armistice Day*

*It was the day
victory was declared in World War I.
Now Veteran's Day honors
all men and women who
have served or are serving
in the military.*

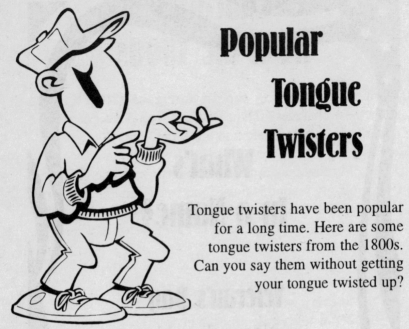

Popular Tongue Twisters

Tongue twisters have been popular for a long time. Here are some tongue twisters from the 1800s. Can you say them without getting your tongue twisted up?

The Twister Twisting

When a twister twisting would twist him a twist,
For twisting his twist three twists he will twist;
But if one of his twists untwists from the twist,
The twist untwisting untwists the twist.

Robert Rowley

Robert Rowley rolled a round roll round;
A round roll Robert Rowley rolled round;
Where rolled the round roll Robert Rowley rolled round?

Charades
from the 1800s

Word games were very popular during the 1800s. Can you solve these charades? (Hint: first and second refer to parts of a word, while whole refers to the entire word.)

1.　　My first makes all nature appear with one face;
　　　At my second is music and beauty and grace;
　　　And if this charade is not easily said,
　　　My whole you deserve to have thrown at your head.

2.　　My first is in most shops;
　　　In every window my second;
　　　My whole is used for the bed,
　　　And, in winter, a comfort is reckoned.

3.　　My first, if you do, you won't hit;
　　　My next, if you do, you won't leave it;
　　　My whole, if you do, you won't guess it.

4.　　My first is always;
　　　My second durable;
　　　My whole without end.

4. Everlasting
3. Mistake
2. Counterpane
1. Snowball
Answers:

87

Great Revivals

Revivals are times when Christians become more committed to their faith and unbelievers are converted in large numbers. While revivals can happen at any time and often happen in small communities, three large revivals during the 1700s and 1800s changed American history.

The Great Awakening

Beginning in the 1720s and reaching its peak in the 1740s, the Great Awakening was the first large revival in the New World. It began in the middle and northern colonies, and Jonathan Edwards was one of its early leaders. Eventually this revival was spread to the south by George Whitefield. Because of the Awakening, people began to believe in revivals and several colleges were founded. Some people argue that the

Great Awakening also created the mind-set needed for American independence.

The Second Awakening

This revival is usually dated from 1800 when camp meetings began to appear. The camp meeting at Cane Ridge, Kentucky, in 1801 was attended by thousands of people and set the pattern for other camp meetings: emotional appeals, a mourner's bench, and periodic meetings. Over the next several years, camp meetings moved East, and Bible camps and conference grounds were established.

At the same time, revival came to the cities and towns of New England, including a series of revivals at Yale University while Timothy Dwight (who happened to be Jonathan Edwards's grandson) was president of the university.

The Awakening of 1857-58

This revival began in New York City in the fall of 1857. It was run by local businessmen and spread to other East Coast and Midwestern cities. Often called the Prayer Meeting Revival, it reached its peak in the spring of 1858 when thousands of people were meeting at noon every day for prayer and testimony. It is estimated that a million members were added to churches because of this revival.

Did You Know...

*The Underground Railroad
was a system for smuggling slaves
out of the South to freedom
before the Civil War.
Often the slaves were sent to
Canada or England.
Not only white northerners,
but also northern blacks and native Americans
helped slaves escape to freedom.*

The Riddler

Riddles have been popular for centuries. Here are some riddles that were popular with children in the 1800s. Can you answer them?

1. Why is a waiter like a racehorse?

2. Why is a clergyman's horse like a king?

3. What is that which lives in winter, dies in summer, and grows with its root upward?

4. Why has Mr. Timothy More, since he lost his hair, become like one of our southern cities?

5. Why is a room full of married folks like an empty room?

6. Why do we all go to bed?

7. Why is an angry person like a loaf?

8. Why is the letter D like a sailor?

9. Why is a theological student like a merchant?

10. Why is an angry man like a lady in full dress?

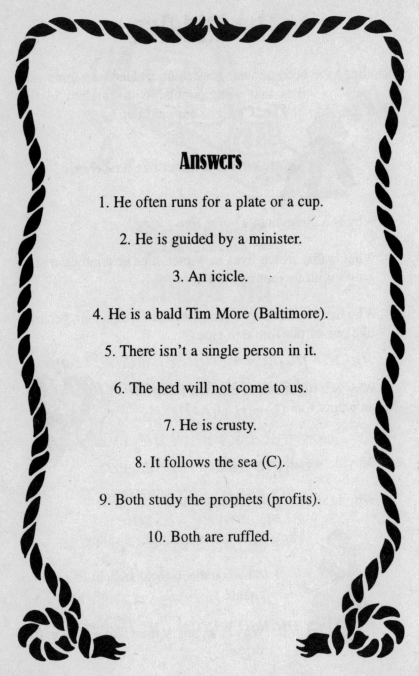

Answers

1. He often runs for a plate or a cup.

2. He is guided by a minister.

3. An icicle.

4. He is a bald Tim More (Baltimore).

5. There isn't a single person in it.

6. The bed will not come to us.

7. He is crusty.

8. It follows the sea (C).

9. Both study the prophets (profits).

10. Both are ruffled.

Plumbing the Depths

Indoor plumbing and toilets were not common in American households until the 1910s, and it wasn't until the 1920s before many homes got access to electricity. This is why the sale of electric appliances such as stoves and irons didn't become a big industry until the 1920s.

Five-Star Generals

Only five people have been named five-star generals in U.S. history. The five-star ranking didn't exist until December 14, 1944 when Congress passed Public Law 482. This is why famous generals like George Washington and Ulysses S. Grant did not have five stars. Five-star generals are also called General of the Army. Here are the five people who have received this honor, along with the date they received it:

George C. Marshall
December 16, 1944

Douglas MacArthur
December 18, 1944

Dwight D. Eisenhower
December 20, 1944

Henry H. Arnold
December 21, 1944
*(General Arnold was later redesignated
General of the Air Force)*

Omar N. Bradley
September 20, 1950

Wars and Casualties

Here is a chart of the major wars
the United States has been involved in
and how many military personnel
were killed in each one.
Combat deaths are people killed in action
or who later died from their wounds.
Other deaths includes:
deaths from disease, hardship,
and accidents.

War	Combat Deaths	Other Deaths
Revolutionary War	4,435	Unknown
Civil War	184,594	373,458
World War I	53,513	63,195
World War II	292,131	115,185
Korean War	33,651	Unknown
Vietnam War	47,369	10,799

Watch Out for... Freckles!

People are often
afraid of new things.
This was certainly true when
electric lights were first introduced.
Critics blamed them for
fires, explosions, and electrocution.

One architect
in the 1880s
even claimed that
using electric light in homes
caused freckles.

Can you match these famous 19th century American authors with the books they wrote?

Louisa May Alcott	The House of Seven Gables
Stephen Crane	Uncle Tom's Cabin
Emily Dickinson	The Prince and the Pauper
Nathaniel Hawthorne	Little Men
Washington Irving	Poems
Herman Melville	The Red Badge of Courage
Edgar Allan Poe	Knickerbocker's History
Harriet Beecher Stowe	Moby Dick
Mark Twain	The Raven

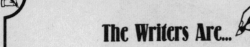

The Writers Are...

Louisa May Alcott
Little Men

Stephen Crane
The Red Badge of Courage

Emily Dickinson
Poems

Nathaniel Hawthorne
The House of Seven Gables

Washington Irving
Knickerbocker's History

Herman Melville
Moby Dick

Edgar Allan Poe
The Raven

Harriet Beecher Stowe
Uncle Tom's Cabin

Mark Twain
The Prince and the Pauper

American Sports Stars

The names of these male sports stars have been written in secret code. Each letter stands for some other letter in the alphabet. Can you break the code and identify these American stars? (Hint, there is a pattern to this code.) Extra credit if you know what sport each man is associated with.

1. CDCH SXQE

2. KHRRH NVHOR

3. KDBJ OLBJIDXR

4. KDBJLH SNCLORNO

5. PLBEDHI KNSADO

6. CDSQ RQDSS

7. QLFHS VNNAR

99

And the Stars Are...

1. Babe Ruth, baseball

2. Jesse Owens, track and field

3. Jack Nicklaus, golf

4. Jackie Robinson, baseball

5. Michael Jordan, basketball

6. Bart Starr, football

7. Tiger Woods, golf

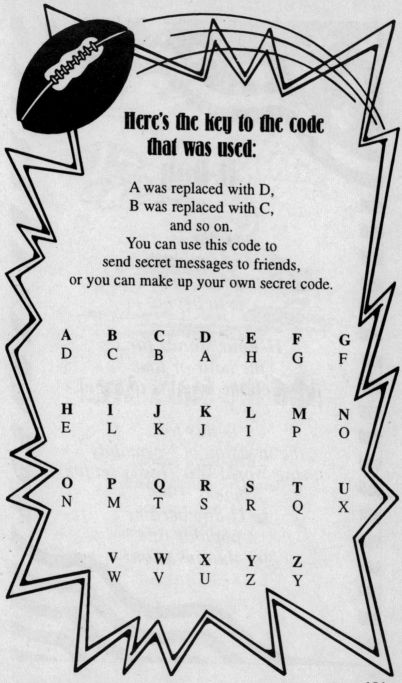

Here's the key to the code that was used:

A was replaced with D,
B was replaced with C,
and so on.
You can use this code to
send secret messages to friends,
or you can make up your own secret code.

A	B	C	D	E	F	G
D	C	B	A	H	G	F

H	I	J	K	L	M	N
E	L	K	J	I	P	O

O	P	Q	R	S	T	U
N	M	T	S	R	Q	X

V	W	X	Y	Z
W	V	U	Z	Y

D-Day

D-day is...
the day on which any
combat attack or operation
is to begin.

H-hour stands for...
the hour or time
at which the event is to begin.

D-day for
the invasion of Normandy
during World War II was set for
June 6, 1944,
so D-day became
a popular title
for that invasion.

Books for ages 7 to 12

Kid Stuff
Fun-filled Activity Books
for ages 7-12

Bible Questions and Answers for Kids
Collection #1 and #2

Brain-teasing questions and answers from the Bible are sure to satisfy the curiosity of any kid. And fun illustrations combined with Bible trivia make for great entertainment and learning! Trade paper; 8 ½" x 11" $2.97 each.

Bible Crosswords for Kids
Collection #1 and #2

Two great collections of Bible-based crossword puzzles are sure to challenge kids ages seven to twelve. Hours of enjoyment and Bible learning are combined into these terrific activity books. Trade paper; 8 ½" x 11" $2.97 each.

The Kid's Book of Awesome Bible Activities
Collection #1 and #2

These fun-filled, Bible-based activity books include challenging word searches, puzzles, hidden pictures, and more! Bible learning becomes fun and meaningful with *The Kid's Book of Awesome Bible Activities*. Trade paper; 8 ½" x 11" $2.97 each.

Available wherever books are sold.
Or order from:
Barbour & Company, Inc.
P.O. Box 719
Uhrichsville, Ohio 44683
http://www.barbourbooks.com

If you order by mail, add $2.00 to your order for shipping. Prices subject to change without notice.

Your Child Is In for the Ultimate American Adventure!

A new book series and fun club for 8-12 year olds! Told through the eyes of kids like yours, *The American Adventure* books will immerse your boy or girl in the action of key events from the *Mayflower* to WWII. Your child will learn America's story and clearly see God's hand throughout our nation's history.

Famous and not-so-famous personalities that have shaped our nation will become living, breathing people. Your child will see how a person's strength of character and depth of conviction influences decisions that impact people, nations, and even the entire world—for hundreds of years.

These kinds of lessons aren't easily learned from typical history books. But in *The American Adventure* books, the lessons are clear, compelling, and unforgettable.

Your first FREE book, *The Mayflower Adventure*, tells of persecution, peril on the ocean, and the excitement of a new land. Mail this coupon today to receive FREE *The Mayflower Adventure*, along with the trial book, *Plymouth Pioneers*. You pay only $3.99 if you choose to keep *Plymouth Pioneers*, or you may return it within 15 days and owe nothing. When you pay for the trial book, your child will be enrolled as a Charter Member of *The American Adventure Club* (includes Member Card, Poster, Stickers, Activity Book, Newsletter, and more) and will receive two new books every month for only $7.98.

You may return any book you're not satisfied with within 15 days and pay nothing, and you may cancel your membership any time. Whatever you decide, *The Mayflower Adventure* is yours to keep. Your child will love it, so act now!

❑ **YES**, send me *FREE The Mayflower Adventure*, and the trial book!

Child's Name_____ Age_____

Parent's Name_____

Address_____

City_____ State_____ Zip_____

Parent Initial Here_____   Adpg97